# The *Essential* School Library Glossary

by Jo Ellen Priest Misakian

Your Trusted
Library-to-Classroom Connection.
Books, Magazines, and Online.

*Dedicated to my dear sister*
*Sharon Kay Priest Robertson (SKPR)*
*"God made us sisters*
*Love made us friends."*

Cataloging-in-Publication Data

Misakian, Jo Ellen Priest.
  The essential school library glossary / Jo Ellen Priest Misakian.
    p. cm.
  ISBN 1-58683-150-X (pbk.)
  1. Library science--Dictionaries. 2. School libraries--Dictionaries. I. Title.
Z1006.M54 2004
020'.3--dc22
                                         2004006746

Author: Jo Ellen Priest Misakian

Linworth Books:
Carol Simpson, Editorial Director
Donna Miller, Editor
Judi Repman, Associate Editor

Published by Linworth Publishing, Inc.
480 East Wilson Bridge Road, Suite L
Worthington, Ohio 43085

Copyright © 2004 by Linworth Publishing, Inc.

All rights reserved. Purchasing this book entitles a librarian to reproduce activity sheets for use in the library within a school or entitles a teacher to reproduce activity sheets for single classroom use within a school. Other portions of the book (up to 15 pages) may be copied for staff development purposes within a single school. Standard citation information should appear on each page. The reproduction of any part of this book for an entire school or school system or for commercial use is strictly prohibited. No part of this book may be electronically reproduced, transmitted, or recorded without written permission from the publisher.

ISBN: 1-58683-150-X

5 4 3 2 1

# Table of Contents

Introduction . . . . . . . . . . . . . . . . . . . . . . . . . . . . . . . . . . . . . . . . . . . . . .v

    A . . . . . . . . . . . . . . . . . . . . . . . . . . . . . . . . . . . . . . . . . . . . . . . . .1
    B . . . . . . . . . . . . . . . . . . . . . . . . . . . . . . . . . . . . . . . . . . . . . . . .11
    C . . . . . . . . . . . . . . . . . . . . . . . . . . . . . . . . . . . . . . . . . . . . . . . .17
    D . . . . . . . . . . . . . . . . . . . . . . . . . . . . . . . . . . . . . . . . . . . . . . . .27
    E . . . . . . . . . . . . . . . . . . . . . . . . . . . . . . . . . . . . . . . . . . . . . . . .31
    F . . . . . . . . . . . . . . . . . . . . . . . . . . . . . . . . . . . . . . . . . . . . . . . .35
    G . . . . . . . . . . . . . . . . . . . . . . . . . . . . . . . . . . . . . . . . . . . . . . . .39
    H . . . . . . . . . . . . . . . . . . . . . . . . . . . . . . . . . . . . . . . . . . . . . . . .41
    I . . . . . . . . . . . . . . . . . . . . . . . . . . . . . . . . . . . . . . . . . . . . . . . .43
    J . . . . . . . . . . . . . . . . . . . . . . . . . . . . . . . . . . . . . . . . . . . . . . . .49
    K . . . . . . . . . . . . . . . . . . . . . . . . . . . . . . . . . . . . . . . . . . . . . . . .51
    L . . . . . . . . . . . . . . . . . . . . . . . . . . . . . . . . . . . . . . . . . . . . . . . .53
    M . . . . . . . . . . . . . . . . . . . . . . . . . . . . . . . . . . . . . . . . . . . . . . .57
    N . . . . . . . . . . . . . . . . . . . . . . . . . . . . . . . . . . . . . . . . . . . . . . . .61
    O . . . . . . . . . . . . . . . . . . . . . . . . . . . . . . . . . . . . . . . . . . . . . . . .63
    P . . . . . . . . . . . . . . . . . . . . . . . . . . . . . . . . . . . . . . . . . . . . . . . .65
    Q . . . . . . . . . . . . . . . . . . . . . . . . . . . . . . . . . . . . . . . . . . . . . . . .69
    R . . . . . . . . . . . . . . . . . . . . . . . . . . . . . . . . . . . . . . . . . . . . . . . .71
    S . . . . . . . . . . . . . . . . . . . . . . . . . . . . . . . . . . . . . . . . . . . . . . . .75
    T . . . . . . . . . . . . . . . . . . . . . . . . . . . . . . . . . . . . . . . . . . . . . . . .81
    U . . . . . . . . . . . . . . . . . . . . . . . . . . . . . . . . . . . . . . . . . . . . . . . .85
    V . . . . . . . . . . . . . . . . . . . . . . . . . . . . . . . . . . . . . . . . . . . . . . . .87
    W . . . . . . . . . . . . . . . . . . . . . . . . . . . . . . . . . . . . . . . . . . . . . . .89
    X . . . . . . . . . . . . . . . . . . . . . . . . . . . . . . . . . . . . . . . . . . . . . . . .91
    Y . . . . . . . . . . . . . . . . . . . . . . . . . . . . . . . . . . . . . . . . . . . . . . . .91
    Z . . . . . . . . . . . . . . . . . . . . . . . . . . . . . . . . . . . . . . . . . . . . . . . .91

List of Acronyms . . . . . . . . . . . . . . . . . . . . . . . . . . . . . . . . . . . . . . .93

# Acknowledgments

I am filled with gratitude for my wonderful family and friends who have supported me during these challenging times of attempting to balance family activities and professional obligations. Special thanks to the ever patient Judi Repman, editor extraordinaire, and to Barbara Currier for sharing her command of technological terminology.

# *Introduction*

Each profession develops and uses its own particular language, the library world being no exception. Terms indigenous to a particular profession are sometimes referred to as jargon. There are several reasons for using profession specific terms. These words and/or phrases can be used within a profession to quickly make a point. It is a venue through which "insiders" can grasp a concept or idea with little discussion.

Profession specific terms can also be used as a tool to impress others. Using terms such as "MARC records" and "action research" conveys our knowledge and understanding of library terminology to the exclusion of those around us. Administrators and others are duly impressed.

When one has worked in and around libraries for a number of years, the jargon makes perfect sense. However, to those entering the profession, the acronyms, words, and terms used by library personnel can be very confusing and tough. It can be extremely frustrating to sit in a room where you perceive those around you to understand the words and/or terms to which the speaker or teacher is referring, but you do not. How many of us have been in this situation? We are reluctant to ask for a definition because we do not want to interrupt the speaker and we may think that everyone else in the room understands perfectly.

Library publications can exacerbate the situation are a glossary or adequate definitions of words and terms within the text are not provided. As a general rule, most popular dictionaries do not provide definitions of words and phrases found in a particular profession's jargon.

The school library media nomenclature consists of not only library jargon, but of school terminology as well. Combining the two professions increases the number of specialized terms. Understanding assessment from a library perspective changes its complexion just a bit. Budgeting takes on a new light in view of library allocations and needs.

This book attempts to provide readers with a resource that will allow quick and easy access to a variety of terms associated with and used by those in the library profession, especially those in the school library media center. It will be particularly useful to students in library school programs at the college or university level who are grappling with many new concepts and ideas. Trying to understand new terminology can add undue stress to challenges associated with unfamiliar and different experiences. This book aims to lower that stress level.

It may be used as a ready reference tool for those working in a school library who may be familiar with a term, but have never actually heard a clear and concise definition of that term. Others may have a need to refresh their knowledge in this area. Those working in a library with little or no formal training should also find this a valuable tool.

Some will find it useful when explaining to others the varied elements of the school library program. Preparing an advocacy presentation often requires a concise definition of a term. Others may have a thorough understanding of a term, but have never had to articulate it in a particularly succinct manner. Sometimes we just need to take a fresh look at terms we intrinsically know, but have not used for a while.

A few of the terms referring to the catalog card may appear to be outdated. They are included for two reasons: 1) some school libraries may not have an automated circulation system and are still using catalog cards, and 2) knowing the structure and purpose of these terms provides a good foundation for knowledge of accepted cataloging practices.

The book is small and inconspicuous; it can accompany you to class along with your textbook or sit quietly on your desk ready for a quick check of a definition of a word or term. The contents are arranged in alphabetical order. Each letter of the alphabet begins a new section and is clearly labeled for easy access. Numerous cross-references are provided and are identified with bold print within certain definitions.

Because the school library media center touches every discipline at the school, it is necessary to produce a publication that reaches beyond the school library. As a result, there are terms in this book that may be specific to other disciplines and professions. For instance, the use of technology figures largely into the library program, so many terms and acronyms pertinent to technology are included within these pages.

I hope you find this book useful, whether you are just entering the profession or are a long-standing member.

**AACR**
See *Anglo-American Cataloging Rules.*

**AACR2**
See *Anglo-American Cataloging Rules*, *2nd edition.*

**AACR2R**
See *Anglo-American Cataloging Rules, 2nd edition, 1988 revision.*

**AACR2 2002**
See *Anglo-American Cataloguing Rules, Second Edition, 2002 Revision (AACR2 2002): The Kit.*

**AASL**
See *American Association of School Librarians.*

**AC**
See *Annotated Card.*

**AECT**
See *Association for Educational Communications and Technology.*

**ASCII**
See *American Standard Code for Information Interchange.*

# A

## Abstract
A synopsis of an article or document usually found at the beginning of scholarly articles; often used to determine if the full text is potentially useful and should be sought. Accessing and downloading abstracts from the **Internet** or an **online database** is sometimes free, while a fee may be charged to access the **full text** of the article or document. Abstracts are typically non evaluative.

## Academic Achievement
**Assessment** of the knowledge level/growth of students, frequently using end-of-grade tests or standardized tests. Some states have designed and implemented state-wide tests to measure academic achievement at the end of a particular grade or for a specific subject. National tests, such as the Iowa Test of Basic Skills, may also be used to measure academic achievement. Growth in some areas of student learning is not easy to assess. For instance, **information literacy skills** are a contributing factor to academic achievement, but are often too complex to isolate on standardized tests, thereby making it difficult to provide a clear link between **information literacy skills** and student achievement. See also: *Assessment*.

## Acceptable Use Policy (AUP)
A statement adopted by schools and libraries that states specific rules for responsible use of the **Internet** and the school district computer **network**. Most schools require this signed agreement between the parent, student, and the school before allowing the student to access and use **Internet resources**.

## Access
The ability of all users to effortlessly and seamlessly locate and use the library materials and **resources** by keeping the library open for student use before, during and after school hours, careful adherence to the **Americans with Disabilities Act (ADA)** to ensure physical access, proper **shelving** and cataloging of materials, instructing students in the use of information **resources**, and having an appropriate selection of materials available for diverse learners.

## Access Point
The **main entry**, added entries, subject entries in a **bibliographic record**, and key words that provide users with information about a specific item. **Author, title**, and subject are the most common access points. **Keyword searching** in an **OPAC** allows users to locate information from various elements of the **bibliographic record**, thereby expanding search results.

# A

## Accession Number

A unique number assigned to each item added to the library collection. Each item is assigned a number or code in consecutive order as it is added to the collection. Automated circulation systems make it unnecessary to assign accession numbers to materials.

## Accountability

Requiring evidence to demonstrate the impact of the library program on student achievement. Accountability methods and strategies should be aligned with national guidelines and state standards. Library personnel should include several methods of accountability, reflecting both **quantitative** and **qualitative** measures.

## Accreditation

A lengthy and detailed investigation to determine the degree to which schools meet the criteria prescribed for a quality educational program. Accreditation is granted at each level of education, K-12 through university, as well as for different programs within the university, through regional, state, and national accreditation bodies. The Western Association of Schools and Colleges (WASC), which investigates secondary and higher education institutions, is an example of a regional agency. State and national agencies accredit universities offering credentials for teachers, **library media specialists**, and administrators. At the national level, the **National Council for the Accreditation of Teacher Education (NCATE)** provides accreditation to colleges of education. The **ALA** accredits those schools and universities offering the MLS or MLIS degree.

## Acquisition

The selection and ordering of library materials. This complex operation requires familiarity with the district/school **curriculum** and community demographics, as well as all policies and procedures for selecting and purchasing library materials. Computer programs have automated many of the technical aspects of the acquisition process. See also: *Selection Policy and Collection Development.*

## Acquisition Policy

A written statement describing the procedures and rationale for purchasing library materials.

## Acquisition Procedures

Describes the steps and specifies the person(s) responsible for ordering library materials. The process involves knowing the district and school's ordering methods, i.e., how to fill out purchase orders and maintain financial records.

### Action Research
The act of gathering and analyzing data to determine the effectiveness of a library media program. **Quantitative** and/or **qualitative** data are used to investigate and supply information on library related issues and concerns. Results should help drive future decisions and offer a rationale for continued support of the library media center program.

### Added Entry
A secondary **access point** on a **catalog** card. **Author** cards are typically considered main entries; subject and **title** cards are added entries. Added entries also provide **access points** for **joint authors**, illustrators, **editors, series,** etc. The **OPAC** allows the use of a variety of **access points** to search for items.

### Adobe Acrobat Reader
A **software** program needed to view **Portable Document Format (PDF)** files. Acrobat Reader may be downloaded free from the **Internet**, but in order to edit PDF documents, the full Adobe Acrobat **software** program must be purchased.

### Advisory Committee
A carefully selected group established to assist in planning activities, establishing policies, and developing short- and long-range goals for the library media center. Members could consist of teachers, staff, parents, administrators, students, and community leaders. This group may become a major advocate for the library program.

### Advocacy
Ongoing activities designed to favorably influence community attitudes toward and perceptions of the library program. This can be accomplished in a variety of ways, i.e., producing library media center newsletters and brochures, making appearances before the board of education, participating in community events, etc.

### Almanac
An **annual** publication containing useful facts and statistical information. Almanacs are used for quickly answering many ready-**reference** type queries. A current version should be in every library.

### American Association of School Librarians (AASL)
A division of the **American Library Association (ALA)**. This is the national association for school library personnel. It provides a variety of services and support to members who enhance the school library program. National conferences are held every other year. *Knowledge Quest* and *School Library Media Research* are publications of AASL.

### American Civil Liberties Union (ACLU)
This association offers support for and publishes materials on citizens' (student) rights and protects **intellectual freedom**. There are ACLU affiliates in every state in the nation.

### American Library Association (ALA)
As the largest library association in America, it provides a wide variety of **resources** and support for academic, public, school, and special libraries. ALA holds two conferences per year: the "Annual" in June or July and "Midwinter" in January or February. The association produces a variety of publications including the **periodical** *American Libraries*.

### American Memory Project
An outreach project of the **Library of Congress (LC)** offering a wealth of **resources**, including **primary source** documents, suggested learning activities, and other information on people and events in American History.

### American Standard Code for Information Interchange (ASCII)
A coding system used to transfer data between different applications and computer **operating systems**. Letters, numbers, punctuation, and other symbols are represented by 128 standard seven-digit **binary** numbers from 0000000 to 1111111.

### Americans with Disabilities Act (ADA)
Mandated by the federal government in 1990, this Act requires that all public services and facilities are easily accessible to people with physical disabilities. School library personnel should make sure the library media center is accessible to all students by considering, among other things, the width of the aisles between the bookshelves and the heights of the **shelving** and tables.

### Analog
Information or signals transmitted in a continuous manner. Analog information must be converted to **digital** format to be read by a computer.

# A

### Anglo-American Cataloging Rules (AACR)
Anglo-American Cataloging Rules, 1st edition. Published in 1967 in Paris, France. AACR outlines the rules for choosing an entry point and the forms of **subject headings**. Because Americans, Canadians, and British representatives could not agree on some **access points**, two separate versions were published.

### Anglo-American Cataloging Rules, 2nd edition (AACR2)
Adopted in 1974, the 2nd edition divides the rules into two parts: 1) the description of library materials, and 2) the **headings**, **uniform titles**, and **access points**. Michael Gorman later created a simplified version titled *The Concise AACR2*.

### Anglo-American Cataloging Rules, 2nd edition, 1988/1998 revisions
Changes and additions in **cataloging** rules continued until this version was published. This **edition** was used in North America and in most English-speaking countries of the world until AACR2 2000 was published.

### Anglo-American Cataloguing Rules, Second Edition, 2002 Revision (AACR2 2002): The Kit
Responding to the rapidly changing types of materials to be cataloged, this new revision of AACR2 comes in loose-leaf format to incorporate into a three-ring binder. Updates are issued annually for inclusion in the binder.

### Annotated Bibliography
A listing of bibliographic information that also includes a short summary of each item. Several standard formats are recommended for producing these documents, i.e., Modern Language Association (MLA), American Psychological Association (APA), and others. See also: **Bibliographic Record**.

### Annotated Card
A **cataloging** program of the **LC** offering **subject headings** more appropriate to materials published for the juvenile market. Some of the *Library of Congress Subject Headings* (**LCSH**) are simplified when the LCSH is not deemed pertinent for a children's library collection, while other headings are added. Annotated card **records** also include summaries of the item.

# A

## Annotation
A description of an item that may also include a critical or subjective **evaluation**. Also indicates the notes added to a **catalog entry**; contents of notes can be searched on an **OPAC** using **keywords**.

## Annual
A specific work published once a year. An example of this would be *The Statesman's Yearbook* or the yearly supplement to an **encyclopedia** set.

## Application Program
Computer **software** designed for performing a specific task, such as word-processing or data management.

## Archival Copy
A non-circulating copy of an item that is usually stored in the library. Use of archival copies is typically restricted and carefully monitored. **Copyright** law permits the creation of an archival (**backup**) copy of computer **software**.

## Archives
A **special collection** of a variety of types of materials that may be of historical value and/or one-of-a-kind items. Items that could not easily be replaced (personal papers, newspaper clippings, photographs, etc.) are often stored in **archives**.

## Art Print
A piece of artwork in the library or classroom, which can be displayed and used for instructional purposes.

## Artifact
An object or **realia** used for instruction or display in the library or classroom. **Primary source** documents like diaries would be examples of artifacts used in classrooms.

## Assessment
Determining the impact of instruction on student learning using a variety of methods, including standardized and other tests, rubrics, and portfolios. Assessment can provide information on the value of the library program and is used to determine the impact of learning activities at the classroom level. See also: *Academic Achievement*.

# A

### Assistive Technology
An item, piece of equipment, or **software** used to improve the functional capabilities of a disabled child or adult. A computer screen with the ability to display text large enough to be read easily by visually impaired students is an example.

### Association for Educational Communications and Technology (AECT)
A national association offering leadership and support in **technology** and communications to the educational community. AECT and **AASL** co-authored *Information Power: Guidelines for School Library Media Programs* and *Information Power: Building Partnerships for Learning* (1988, 1998).

### Asynchronous
Occurring at different times. In **online** learning asynchronous refers to a discussion where participants log on at different times to participate in an ongoing discussion. This is the opposite of **synchronous**, in which two or more people participate in an **online** discussion at the same time.

### Atlas
A published **volume**—usually oversized—containing a series of maps of the world, countries, or states. It can be all encompassing or focus on different aspects of the geographical world, such as political, historical, or thematic.

### Audio-Visual Materials
**Resources** that use sound, text, and imagery to provide information on a particular subject. These non-book materials, audiotapes, CDs, **DVD**s, videotape, etc., require some kind of additional equipment in order to be used.

### Authentic Learning
Student-centered instruction that fosters questioning and thinking processes that propel students toward the acquisition of skills which enable them to identify a real-life problem and then locate, evaluate, and use information to solve that problem. See also: *Independent Learning*.

### Authentication
Computer verification of the identity of an individual or computer through a username and password, which permits access to a particular **network** and/or data.

# A

## Author
The intellectual or artistic creator of a work; commonly attributed to the writer(s) of a book or article. An author can be one or more persons, a governmental agency, company, or professional organization.

## Author Card
A rectangular piece of stiff paper in the **catalog** drawer with the **author's** name on the top line. It is usually the **main entry card**.

## Authority
The knowledge, abilities, and intelligence attributed to the creator and/or **editor** of a work. Authority is a major consideration when judging the value of a work. This is an especially important consideration when determining the value of **Internet resources**.

## Authority Control
Rules that dictate the verbal form that **subject headings**, **uniform titles**, and **author** entries take and determine how they are entered into a **bibliographic record**. It assures consistency in assigning **headings** and demonstrates the relationship between names, works, and subjects.

## Authority File
A group of **records** containing the chosen form of names, subjects, **titles**, and **series** used in the **catalog** of that library, such as the **LCSH** or *Sears List of Subject Headings (Sears)*. **Access** is enhanced when uniform rules are used to create a **bibliographic record**.

## Automation System
A computer **software** program that streamlines many of the tasks associated with operating a library. A good automation **software** system can perform such tasks as ordering and tracking materials, providing pertinent data connected with the collection and **patrons**, checking in and out materials, preparing overdue lists and notices, etc. It also provides **access** to the collection via the **OPAC**.

### BIP
See *Books in Print*.

### Backorder
A materials purchase request that a wholesaler, **jobber**, or **vendor** is not able to fulfill at the time an order is placed. The supplier typically notifies the customer that the item is not available for shipment, but may be supplied at a later date. Personnel must then decide if it is desirable to wait for the material(s) or cancel the order.

### Backup
A system, device, or program used to save computer data in case of **hardware** or **software** failure. Most libraries perform a backup of their circulation data at the end of each day using a tape, **CD-ROM**, **DVD**, or other **media**.

### Bandwidth
The amount of data that can be transmitted over a **network**. Bandwidth is measured in **bits**, megabits, **megabytes**, or **gigabytes** per second. The higher the bandwidth, the faster the transmission speed.

# B

## Barcode

A horizontal strip or label consisting of vertical lines and spaces of varying width, found on either the front or back inside or outside covers of library books and **patron records** (library cards). The labels are scanned into and read by a computer when materials are inventoried and/or checked in and out of the library. They are also used for identification and record-keeping of library materials and **patrons**.

## Behaviorism

Learning theory prescribing that teachers maintain a closely monitored and structured learning environment in the classroom. In 1949, Ralph Tyler described principles of identifying the needs of the learner, setting learning objectives, designing activities, and evaluating outcomes. This theory presents a particular challenge to **library media specialists** who ascribe to the **Constructivist** theory of a student-centered learning environment.

## Bi-Annual

A publication issued twice a year.

## Bibliographic Record

A **catalog entry** that describes a specific resource. The bibliographic record may include the **call number**, **author**, **title**, place of publication, **publisher**, **subject headings**, date, **edition**, pages, and illustrations. The **record** may be created in many formats including a print **catalog** card or electronic data.

## Bibliographic Tools

Books, **journals**, **indexes**, **catalogs**, and **online resources** used for selecting and ordering library materials. The tools vary in depth and breadth of purpose. Some provide information on the price and availability of items, while others include an **evaluation** of the material. *Books in Print* is a nonevaluative bibliographic tool, while *Children's Catalog* evaluates items included in its entries.

## Bibliographic Utility

A system that provides **access** to large bibliographic **databases** for **cataloging** purposes. It can be a cooperative venture, such as **Online Computer Library Center (OCLC)**, the **Research Libraries Information Network (RLIN)**, or a commercial product, such as Alliance Plus.

## Bibliography

A list of **citations**, **references**, or **resources** usually found at the end of a paper, article, or book identifying the **resources** used within that work. Bibliographies may also be stand-alone documents focusing on a particular theme, **author**, or reading level(s). Information within the **citation** may include an **annotation** and/or an **evaluation** of the item(s).

## Biennial

A **serial** publication issued every two years.

## Big6

An information problem-solving model designed to teach **information literacy skills** to students at all levels. The co-creators of the Big6 are Dr. Michael Eisenberg and Bob Berkowitz. See also: *Information Process Models*.

## Bi-Monthly

A publication issued six times a year.

## Binary

Numbers in base 2, consisting entirely of zeroes and ones. Normally we use base 10 with the digits 0-9. The binary number system is used by computer scientists because zero and one can be translated to current on or current off.

## Bindery

An operation or business that binds or rebinds periodicals and books, usually in hard cover, to improve or extend the life of the item.

## Biography

A chronicle of the life of an individual.

## Bit

An abbreviation for **binary** digit, a zero or one, the smallest unit of information in a computer's memory. Letters are formed in the computer using combinations of zeros and ones.

## Bi-Weekly

A publication issued two times a month or every other week.

# B

## Blanket Order
A materials order placed with a particular **vendor** or **publisher** that stipulates the purchase of all items of a particular nature. Some school libraries submit a blanket order for all materials ordered in a certain subject area.

## Blog
Short for weB LOG. A Web page used primarily as a journal for an individual, usually centered on the opinions and concerns of that person. Often updated daily, it may offer editorial or personal information and contain collections of links to various other **Web sites**.

## Bluetooth
Technology that allows devices that would normally be plugged into a computer to be connected wirelessly. The devices so equipped allow the computer to function as a personal- area network (PAN) providing links between the computer, mobile phones and other portable handheld devices and the Internet.

## Blurb
A synopsis of the contents of a book, usually found on the **book jacket**.

## Board of Trustees
The governing body of a school district that sets policies and procedures, settles disputes, and conducts other business necessary for the operation of a school district. May also be known as a Board of Education.

## Book Editor
The person who works with an **author** to prepare a **manuscript** for publication by making revisions and offering suggestions for improvement.

## Book Jacket
A paper covering placed on a book to protect the binding.

## Book Review
A written **evaluation** of a book. Most commonly refers to a published review.

## Books in Print (BIP)
A list of books currently **in print** and available for ordering. The most definitive **annual** publication providing bibliographic information on items **in print** is Bowker's *Books in Print*. It is available in print, **CD-ROM**, and **online**.

## Booktalking

A method of enticing others to read a particular book or books. The prospective reader is convinced to read the book when supplied with just enough information about the plot to motivate interest. Booktalks can be about individual books or based on a theme or **genre**. They can be performed informally one-on-one or more formally to a large group.

## Boolean Searching

Named for mathematician George Boole (1815-1864), Boolean is a **search strategy** (logic) that facilitates the **location** of items using **keyword searching** by employing the terms (operators), AND, OR, and NOT. It permits expanding the search (OR) by searching for either term, limiting the search (AND) by using both terms, or eliminating a particular term from the search (NOT).

## Budget

A financial plan for spending money allocated to the library program for a fiscal year. Libraries may have a variety of funding sources, which must be carefully tracked. A well-planned budget is necessary in order to assure responsible purchasing. May also be used as a tool to demonstrate the needs of the library program.

## Budgetary Process

The development of a detailed and carefully designed **budget** for the library program. It includes assessing needs, setting goals, providing justification, and evaluating the appropriateness of expenditures.

## Byte

A collection of **binary** digits used to compose letters, numerals, or symbols in a microcomputer. A byte is composed of **bits**, the smallest unit of information that can be accessed on a computer. Common sizes of bytes include 8, 16, and 32 **bits**, the most common being 8 **bits**.

### CD-ROM

An acronym for Compact Disk-Read-Only-Memory. This 12cm disc can store thousands (about 300,000) of pages of information that can be read by a computer. Data cannot be added to a "Read Only" disc.

### CIP

See *Cataloging in Publication*.

### CPU

See *Central Processing Unit*.

### CRL

See *Center for Research Libraries*.

### Cache

A storage area in computer memory that temporarily stores frequently accessed data, such as the **Internet** sites you have recently visited. The **Web sites** held here load more quickly than other sites. To conserve memory, the **browser's** cache empties itself periodically as dictated by **software** settings.

# C

## Call Number

The unique combination of numbers and letters used for classifying and locating a particular item in the library. Call numbers group works by subject/discipline or by **genre**. Each call number consists of several lines: a **classification number** or a letter (F for Fiction, E for easy or everybody, B for **Biography**, etc.). The **classification number** or letter is followed by a **Cutter Number** or **author** number, usually the first two or three letters of the **author's** last name. Some libraries add a **location** indicator (AV for audio-visual materials, CS for computer **software**) before the **classification number** or letter. The **Dewey Decimal Classification (DDC)** system is used to produce a **classification number** in most school library media centers. Academic and other large libraries often use the **Library of Congress Classification (LCC)** system. See also: *Classification Number*.

## Camcorder

A self-contained videotape recording device capable of recording live signals through a video or antenna signal. Combines the features of a video camera and a videocassette recorder.

## Card Catalog

The **index** to all materials in the school library media center, in card form. Filed alphabetically by the information on the top line of each card. Items usually have **title, author,** and **subject cards**. Because of the capabilities of the computer, many libraries now use the **OPAC** in lieu of the physical card catalog.

## Catalog

A list of materials in a particular library or group of libraries describing the **holdings** in that library. In early libraries, the lists were kept in a book(s); later, the **records** were moved to the **card catalog**. Today, most catalogs are created using a **software** system that permits **access** to the collection via the **OPAC**, which may also provide **access** via the **Internet**.

## Cataloging

The process of creating a unique **bibliographic record** for each item in the library. Cataloging involves describing a work, performing subject analysis, and assigning a **classification number**. Correct and complete catalog **records** ensure that the library collection is easily accessible to **patrons**. See also: *Descriptive Cataloging and Subject Cataloging*.

# C

## Cataloging in Publication (CIP)
An agreement between the **LC** and American **publishers** that provides pre-publication **cataloging** information, typically printed on the **verso** of the **title page** of print **resources**. CIP can be used for **copy cataloging** by completing and checking the information based on the item as published.

## Censorship
The process of removing or suppressing what is considered morally, politically, or otherwise offensive to an individual or group. **ALA** promotes free **access** for all citizens and is opposed to censorship. The Office of Intellectual Freedom of **ALA** supplies a variety of information and support to libraries facing challenges with library materials.

## Center for Research Libraries (CRL)
A non-profit international consortium of colleges, universities, and libraries that offers its members **access** to a variety of **research** options and **resources**.

## Central Processing Unit (CPU)
The "brains" of the computer, where the logic, arithmetic, and control units are located and where computations, comparisons, and sorting functions occur. It directs and coordinates the activities of the computer.

## Charter Schools
A public school formed by a group or organization operating under a more flexible structure than that of a traditional public school. Charter schools are often exempt from certain state department of education requirements.

## Chief Source of Information
Designated location on an item specifying the bibliographic information used for creating the **catalog record**. The location of the information varies depending on the type of material. The chief source of information for a book is the **title page** and the **verso** of the title page. **AACR2** specifies where to locate the chief source of information on materials in different formats.

## Children's Catalog
An H.W. Wilson publication that includes an extensive list of high quality materials for children. This resource is widely used as a general selection tool. Others in the **series** are *Middle and Junior High School Library Catalog,* and *Senior High School Library Catalog*. All are now available in electronic format and **online**.

# C

### Circulation Card
A unique paper kept in the book pocket until the item is checked out by **patrons**, who must write their name on it before submitting the item for check out. It is then kept in the library as a record of who borrowed the item and when it is to be returned. In most libraries, this has been replaced by computerized circulation systems, which rely on **barcode** scanning for linking the **patron** to the borrowed item.

### Circulation Desk
The place where the business of circulating library items is conducted. **Patrons** can check out, return, renew, and/or place a hold on items. **Patrons** may also ask about the status of particular library materials, seek help locating material, and request **reference** assistance at the circulation desk.

### Circulation System
A **software** application that allows materials to be checked in and out of the library, as well as permits accurate record keeping and generation of reports. **Circulation system software** interfaces with **OPAC software** to provide **access** to the collection.

### Citation
The bibliographic information usually found at the end of **journal** articles or books, giving recognition and credit to the creator of the article or citing information, referred to in the body of the work. Citations also help users locate the source(s) referenced in the publication and can be used for locating additional information on the topic.

### Classification
The organization of knowledge, usually by discipline or subject, in a library. Schools and many public libraries use the **DDC**, while libraries with very large collections use the **LCC** system.

### Classification Number
The number assigned to a resource that indicates its primary subject and determines its relative placement in the library. See also: *Call Number*.

### Client
A computer that receives information or services by connecting to a **server**.

## Closed Circuit
A system of transmitting and receiving television signals using equipment directly linked by coaxial cable, microwave, or telephone lines.

## Code of Ethics
A set of mores that dictate expected behavior within a profession. **ALA** provides a code of ethics specifically for **librarians/library media specialists**. It can be viewed **online** at <www.ala.org/alaorg/oif/ethics.html>.

## Collaboration
Classroom teachers and **library media specialists** working together to design, teach, and evaluate a unit of study. The **library media specialist** may use this venue to introduce and teach the **Information Literacy Standards for Student Learning** to students and classroom teachers.

## Collaborative Planning
The joint effort between a classroom teacher and a library media teacher to design a **curriculum** unit or lesson.

## Collaborative Teaching
The joint effort between a classroom teacher and a library media teacher to deliver instruction. The classroom teacher and the library media teacher each play an instructional role. For example, the classroom teacher assigns and teaches the content while the **library media specialist** guides students to **access**, evaluate, synthesize, and use a wide array of **resources**. Collaborative teaching uses a variety of techniques, materials, and **assessments** to develop information-literate students.

## Collation
The physical description of an item within the **cataloging record**. It may include noting the number of pages, **volumes** and illustrations.

## Collection Development
An ongoing systematic process to identify the strengths and weaknesses of the library collection and identify materials for **acquisition**. Continuous assessment of the community, the collection, and the **curriculum** is necessary in order to acquire appropriate **resources**.

# C

## Collection Mapping

A strategy for conducting an analysis of the library media collection. This includes examining the **resources** in terms of their age and their relevancy to the informational needs and reading interests of the school community. A carefully designed and prepared "map" of the **resources** provides a clear picture of the strengths and weaknesses of the library collection.

## Collocation

Bringing related works together such as those by the same **author** and of the same subject both on the library shelves and in the **catalog**. For instance, **patrons** searching for books by Mark Twain, a pseudonym, will also be guided to works published under the **author's** real name, Samuel Clemens, using the **See** and **See Also** reference. The **DDC** system brings disciplines together on the library shelves.

## Colophon

An identifying mark sometimes located at the end of a book, which often includes information on the typeface or printer used in publishing the book.

## Community Resources

Sources outside of the immediate school setting that can be utilized for instructional purposes. For example, community members may be interviewed, which would be considered a **primary source** when doing **research**. Local service organizations may be tapped for a variety of support materials and activities for the school library media program.

## Competencies

Specified levels of academic performance. Many states have identified and adopted a sequence of competencies across subjects and grade levels. A variety of **assessment** tools are used to determine mastery of competencies.

## Compression

A process of digitizing information to reduce the amount of **bandwidth** or **bits** required, thereby facilitating faster transmission of data over a **network** or the **Internet**.

## Computer-Assisted Instruction (CAI)

Computer **software** designed for instruction (drill and practice, tutorials, simulations, or educational games). CAI is used to increase skills or knowledge in a specific curricular area.

# C

## Consideration File
A list of materials for future library purchases, sometimes referred to as a "wish list".

## Constructivist Teaching
An instructional theory derived from **research** in cognitive psychology. It asserts that human beings develop concepts through their own intellectual interactions with and actions upon their world. Learners are not passive, but are actively engaged in their own learning through a variety of methods. **Information literacy skills** instruction is rooted in the Constructivist theory.

## Content Standards
Prescribe **competencies** students are expected to master in each grade level and are dictated by the state in which the students reside. Content standards have also been developed by subject specialty associations associated with K-12 education such as the National Council of the Teachers of Mathematics and the National Council for the Social Studies. **AASL** and **AECT** developed the **Information Literacy Standards** for Student Learning. Local, state or national standardized tests are used to determine mastery of the standards.

## Continuum of Information Skills
A school or districtwide **curriculum** of **information literacy competencies** designed to develop skills from basic to complex. Information skills introduced early in the student's educational experiences are built upon and reinforced at each grade level until mastery occurs.

## Controlled Vocabulary
A list of terms used for indexing and searching. An example would be a **subject heading** list (*Sears* and **LCSH**) or a **thesaurus**.

## Cookie
A small file sent by a **Web site** to the viewer's **browser** that retains information until that site is visited again and is then sent back to the site. It may contain registration information, "shopping cart" information, user preferences, and other pertinent information.

## Copy Cataloging
Creating a **cataloging record** based on an existing one. The existing **catalogs** most commonly used for this purpose are the **CIP record**, the **OCLC**, and the **RLIN**. This is in lieu of creating original **cataloging** within one's own library. See also: **Original Cataloging**.

# C

## Copy Editor
The person who makes sure a **manuscript** is clearly and accurately written prior to publication.

## Copy Number
An individual number used to identify specific items when multiple copies of one **title** are in the library collection.

## Copyright
The exclusive rights granted to the creator of a work to publish or sell his/her material for a specified number of years. Copyright laws were enacted to protect the creator of a work. The **Fair Use** section of the Act was created for the purpose of permitting copyrighted works to be used in educational settings by following specific guidelines.

## Copyright Date
A date on material indicating when it was granted official **copyright** protection. The copyright date is usually found on the back (**verso**) of the **title page** of a book and on various parts of other **media**. The symbol © proceeds the date on which the work was copyrighted. Since 1986, a **copyright** notice is no longer required to protect a work under **copyright** law.

## Corporate Body
Associations, businesses, institutions, or organizations are identified as part of an **entry** in a **bibliographic record**.

## Critical Thinking
Instructional approaches designed to lead students to think creatively and deeply about an issue and gain an understanding of that issue, through specific learning experiences.

## Cross-Reference
A reference to another subject or to additional subjects (**See also** reference). Cross-references guide the user to additional **resources** for locating information on a particular subject, time, place, or person.

## Curriculum
The topical sequence of study adopted by a school, district, and/or state designed to build upon knowledge and skills across grade levels.

## Curriculum Development
A systematic process designed, developed, and used to assess the needs and capabilities of the learner and to select or create instructional materials and activities to foster learning.

## Curriculum Integration
The relationship between **curriculum** content, **information literacy skills** instruction, and **technology**-based instructional materials. Information skills and materials in all formats are seamlessly integrated into the school's existing **curriculum**.

## Curriculum Mapping
Aligning materials in the school library with the school **curriculum**. This "map" will uncover the strengths and weaknesses in the library's collection in relation to the school's **curriculum**. The curriculum mapping process can be used to supply justification for future purchases.

## Cutter Number
Added to the **classification number**, it is an alphanumeric scheme to designate the **author** or **main entry**. It is derived from the Cutter or Cutter-Sanborn tables. Today, Cutter numbers are usually replaced with the first three letters of the **author's** last name.

## Cyberspace
Coined by **author** William Bibson in his novel *Neuromancer*, the term refers to all information available over computer **networks**.

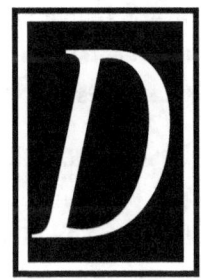

### DVD
See *Digital Video Disc*.

### Data Analysis
Examination and **evaluation** of data collected in relation to the purposes of the library media program, services, and **resources**.

### Database
A collection of electronic **records** created by and accessible with computer **software**. **Bibliographic records** are entered into an **electronic database** for manipulation and **access** in an automated circulation system.

### Debugging
Locating and correcting errors in a computer program or file.

### Delimiter
In a **Machine Readable Cataloging (MARC) record,** this is represented by a symbol indicating the start of a **subfield. Software** programs use different symbols to indicate a delimiter, i.e., ≠ or @. The symbol would be used to divide the **subfield** into, for example, the size and number of pages.

# D

## Depository
A library that agrees to retain certain materials and make them available to the general public. U.S. federal and United Nations documents are examples of **resources** held in depositories.

## Descriptive Cataloging
The procedure of identifying and physically describing an item, identifying the **access points**, and recording the information in a **bibliographic record**.

## De-Selecting Library Materials
A term used when **weeding** the library collection to refer to the discarding of out-of-date and irrelevant library materials. See also: *Weeding*.

## Desktop Publishing
Computer **software** that allows the integration of text and graphics to produce high quality documents for publication.

## Dewey Decimal Classification (DDC)
The system of categorizing and organizing library materials using the decimally divisible table of numbers devised by Melvil E. Dewey. Ten categories are used to classify human knowledge. The structure is widely used and easily understood by **patrons**.

## Dial-Up Internet Connection
A **hardware** device that allows a user to connect to an **Internet Service Provider (ISP)** using a **modem** and a telephone line to **access** and browse the **Internet/World Wide Web (WWW)** and to send and receive electronic mail (**email**).

## Digital
A method of converting various media into a format, consisting of a sequence of numbers allows data to be manipulated and displayed on a computer and other devices. Digital technology is rapidly replacing **analog technology**. See also: *Analog*.

## Digital Projector
A **hardware** device that receives data in several possible forms (**digital**, S-Video, RCA), enlarges it, and projects it with a lamp through an adjustable lens onto a flat surface, such as a screen acting as a large monitor. Can be used to present images or text from a connected computer, **DVD** player, VCR, television, or other media.

## Digital Video Disc (DVD)
An optical medium on which music, data, film, and **software** can be stored and accessed using the appropriate **software** and equipment. It holds more data than a **CD-ROM**.

## Digitization
The conversion of print, audio, or video **resources** to **digital** form which can then be accessed and manipulated using computer **software**.

## Dissertation
A treatise or **thesis** written by a candidate for a doctoral degree.

## Distance Learning/Education
A method of instruction and learning that allows students to **access** and respond to instruction though **telecommunications**. **Online** teaching and learning is rapidly replacing other methods of distance education delivery because it permits interaction to be **asynchronous** or **synchronous** and allows students to **access** a wide range of instructional materials in different formats.

## Document Delivery
A service allowing users to order copies of documents, such as **journal** articles from a remote library or commercial provider. See also: **Interlibrary Loan**.

## Domain Name
The classification that identifies a computer's **IP number** within the **Internet** world. Located at the end of a **Web site** address, it indicates whether it is a commercial, non-profit, educational, or governmental site. For instance, .org stands for non-profit organization; .com for commercial enterprises; .edu for educational institutions; and .gov for governmental agencies

## Dot-Matrix Printer
An impact printer that works much like a typewriter: a head tapping dots onto the paper though a ribbon.

## ERIC

See *Educational Resources Information Center.*

## Edition

All copies of a **title** issued by the same **publisher** that contain the same content. If the text has been changed or additions made when subsequent copies are published, a new or revised edition is noted and indicated in the **cataloging record** and on the **verso** of the **title page**.

## Editor

The person who collaborates with an **author** or agency to help prepare a **manuscript** for publication.

## Educational Resources Information Center (ERIC)

A U.S. Department of Education project that provides full-text, **abstracts**, bibliographies, and other products on a variety of topics of particular interest to the educational community.

## Electronic Database

**Records** created in or converted to an electronic format that can be accessed and manipulated using a computer **software** program.

# E

### Electronic Journal
A **journal** produced or converted into an electronic format, available **online** or on a **CD-ROM**.

### Electronic Portfolio
A professional dossier produced in an electronic format that can be mounted on the **Web, CD-ROM,** or **DVD**. This is gaining in popularity as a method for presenting professional dossiers. They are also becoming a common way for K-12 students to show growth and progress over a course of instructional time.

### Electronic Resources
Materials that can be accessed and used from **resources** other than print.

### Elementary and Secondary Education Act (ESEA)
First enacted in 1968, this program provides federal money for educational purposes. In many districts, school libraries have been the recipient of some or all of this funding.

### eMail
An abbreviation for electronic mail that is used to send messages from one computer to another via the **Internet**.

### Encryption
The encoding of information so as to ensure a private transmission. The message is encoded accorded to a data encryption standard (DES).

### Encyclopedia
A general **reference** source containing brief or lengthy information on a variety of topics. They can also be specific to a particular discipline, such as science or art.

### Entry
A **record** of an item found in the library **catalog** or in an **index**.

### Errata
The errors discovered after the publication of an item. Corrections are included with or attached to the item.

## Ethernet

A **local area network (LAN)** connecting computers of various types by using a common **protocol**. Enables those on the **network** to **access** and use a variety of information and **resources**.

## Ethics

Moral values and rules of conduct. Every profession has a set of standards for ethical behavior. Library personnel subscribe to the **ALA Code of Ethics**. See also: *Code of Ethics*.

## Evaluation

The process of identifying a need or problem and establishing methods of **assessment**, then collecting, analyzing, interpreting the data, and reporting the findings. School libraries can and should make use of this process to build a high-quality library media program. Data gathered through the evaluation process may convey the impact of the program on student learning. See also: *Accountability and Assessment*.

## FTP
See *File Transfer Protocol.*

## Fair Use
Under **copyright** law, some exceptions are in place for certain uses of copyrighted materials. Section 107 of the Copyright Act of 1976 provides guidelines for the fair use of copyrighted materials. The four Fair Use requirements include 1) the purpose and character of the use, 2) the nature of the copyrighted work, 3) the amount and substantiality of the portion used, and 4) the effect of the use upon the potential market of the work. This means that in schools a certain amount of information, within Fair Use parameters, can be shared with students in a classroom or library. Details on this section of the Act can be found at <http://www.copyright.gov/title17/92chap1.html#107>. The Copyright Office **home page** can be accessed at <http://www.copyright.gov/>.

## Fax
Short for telefacsimile, which is the speedy transmission and reception, via **telecommunication** devices, of the exact replica of a printed page.

## Fiber Optics
Long, thin strands of glass transmitting information on modulated light beams, through which a large amount of data can be quickly transmitted and received.

# F

### Field
The part of a **database record** that identifies a particular piece of information, such as an **author, title,** or subject field, in **cataloging records** and **database** files. In **MARC records**, each field is represented by a three-digit **tag**, which identifies the type of data to follow. **Indicators** and **subfield codes** further define the **records** within a field.

### File Transfer Protocol (FTP)
The computer code/instructions used to transmit electronic files from one computer to another via **telecommunications software**.

### Fine
The cost charged to a borrower for lost or delinquent library materials. District policy guides the assessment of fines; some schools charge for lost materials, but not for late items.

### Firewall
**Software** that prevents unauthorized access to a computer or **server**. Most school systems maintain this block to prevent unauthorized access to the **network**.

### Firewire
High-speed computer serial interface with high bandwidth, suitable for digital video, digital still cameras, and home entertainment devices.

### Flexible Scheduling
A plan allowing students **access** to the library and its **resources** at point of need. This contrasts with fixed scheduling, where classes are scheduled to use the library following a pre-set schedule.

### Floppy Disk
An inexpensive, thin magnetic storage disk encased in stiff plastic. Holds a relatively small amount of data.

### Foreword
Typically found at the beginning of a book, it provides some history or background information on how and why the book was written. May be written by the **author**, but is frequently written by another, sometimes more prominent, person to promote or validate the content.

# F

### Free Voluntary Reading
A term coined by Dr. Stephan Krashen, USC Emeritus Professor, to indicate the positive impact of offering young people lots of books, **magazines**, comic books, or whatever is of interest to them to read. Dr. Krashen has conducted and reported on **research** that substantiates the theory that setting aside time for pleasurable reading and having an abundance of books encourages more frequent reading, leading to increased reading skills.

### The Freedom to Read
A statement that supports and defends the First Amendment right of free expression. **ALA** offers legal counsel and other services to libraries and **librarians** in support of this Amendment. **ALA**'s statement can be found at <http://www.ala.org/Content/NavigationMenu/Our_Association/Offices/Intellectual_Freedom3/Statements_and_Policies/Freedom_to_Read_Statement/Freedom_to_Read_Statement.htm>.

### Freeware
Openly available **software**. **Copyright** is retained by the developer who offers its use for free or for a minimal charge, under certain restrictions. Usually downloaded from the **Internet**.

### Full Text
An **online** or electronic resource providing the complete contents of an article, as opposed to the abbreviated **abstract**. The term usually indicates that the entire article can be accessed and downloaded from an electronic source.

### Full-Motion Video
A film that plays at the rate of 30 frames per second.

### Function Keys
Specific manual input device on a computer keyboard programmed to quickly perform a defined task. Tapping just one such key would direct the computer to save, copy, paste, or send a file.

### GIF
See *Graphics Interchange Format.*

### Gazetteer
A geographical dictionary that provides a wide array but brief geographic information, such as names of places, locations, statistical information, and physical descriptions.

### General Material Designation (GMD)
In a **cataloging record**, this identifies the class of material to which the item belongs. **AACR2R** provides standard terms to be used for specific items. For instance, when **cataloging** a movie, one would use the term "motion picture." If no designation is given, it usually refers, by default, to a book.

### Genre
Typically refers to a kind or type of literature containing a common set of characteristics, such as fantasy or science fiction.

### Gigabyte
One billion **bytes**.

# G

### Glossary
An alphabetical listing of definitions of terms specific to a particular subject/discipline, typically located within a book.

### Government Document
A publication produced and issued by federal, state, or local governmental agencies and made available to the public via a variety of methods, such as print, **depository** libraries, or the **Internet**.

### Graphics Interchange Format (GIF)
A method used to compress images.

## HTML
See *Hypertext Markup Language*.

## http
See *Hypertext Transfer Protocol*.

## Hacker
A person who attempts illegal entry into a private computer system.

## Hard Copy
The print copy of an item as opposed to the **digital** copy or image displayed on a computer screen.

## Hardware
The term for a computer or other pieces of technological equipment.

## Heading
The first line of a **cataloging record** or **index** indicating either the **author**, subject, **title**, or some other distinguishing feature. See also: *Access Point*.

## Holdings
Materials owned by a particular library, including all print and nonprint **resources**.

# H

## Home Page

The introductory page of a **Web site**. It usually includes **hypertext links** to other sites containing additional information.

## Hypertext Link

A word or phrase in a computerized document that, when clicked on by the user, transparently links to another **Web** page or resource.

## Hypertext Markup Language (HTML)

The scripting language, or set of rules and **tags**, describing the structure of a document for display on **Web** pages. Specific symbols are used so a document will retain its proper form when published on a **Web** page. For instance, a <P> is used to begin a paragraph and </P> to end it. The symbols <I> and </I> surrounding a word or phrase tell the computer to italicize that portion of the document. Some **software** programs perform this function by allowing documents to be saved in HTML.

## Hypertext Transfer Protocol

The standard used to transfer data over the World Wide Web. It is used to send a request to an appropriate Web server, enabling the computer to access HTML pages.

## IASL
See *International Association of School Librarianship.*

## ILL
See *Interlibrary Loan.*

## ISBD
See *International Standard Bibliographic Description.*

## ISBN
See *International Standard Book Number.*

## ISSN
See *International Standard Serial Number.*

## ISTE
See *International Society for Technology in Education.*

## I-Search
A **research** process developed in 1988 by Ken Macrorie, who felt that students would compose higher quality and more comprehensively written material when researching and writing about topics of personal interest.

# I

## IP Number
A four-part number, separated by dots, assigned to a specific computer to allow it to connect to the **Internet** from within a particular **network**.

## Ibid
An abbreviation for the Latin term *ibiden*, meaning "in the same place." It is used in **citations** and **references** to prevent retyping the **author** or **title** of the previous **entry**.

## Icon
A picture used in a graphical interface to represent a program or link. Positioning the cursor over the graphic or picture and clicking on the mouse button will open a **software application program** or take one to a particular **Internet** site.

## Impression
All copies of a particular **edition** printed at the same time.

## Imprint
A mark on an item that displays the **publisher** or producer's name and date of publication.

## In Print
A term used to convey that a particular book is currently in print and available for purchase from the **publisher** or a **jobber**. See also: *Out of Print*.

## Independent Learning
To initiate one's own learning and become self-reliant and self-directed. Classroom teachers and **library media specialists**, who collaboratively design the **curriculum** and instruction centered around the student, enable students to "learn how to learn." See also: *Resource-Based Learning*.

## Index
An alphabetical list that offers a guide to specific contents within a particular document or resource. At the end of a book, it points the reader to a particular piece of information in the book. Stand-alone indices provide bibliographic analysis of the contents of groups of periodicals. Indices can be **in print** or electronic form and are usually arranged by subject, **author**, or **title**.

# I

## Indicators

In the **MARC** format, this symbol can be identified by two one-digit numeric codes defining how to process information within a **field**. For instance, the first indicator may tell the computer there should be a **title entry** for that item. The second indicator directs the computer to disregard a certain number of nonfiling characters, such as "the," "a," and spaces, when entering the **title** of that item.

## Information Literacy

The ability to recognize an information need and know how to use specific strategies to answer a question or solve a problem. An information literate person will understand the information-seeking process and use it to locate, evaluate, synthesize, use, and produce information, using a variety of **resources** and **media**.

## Information Literacy Skills

Techniques and strategies taught by the **library media specialist** in **collaboration** with the classroom teacher that enable students to **access**, evaluate, and use information to create new knowledge and understanding.

## Information Literacy Standards

Nine principles for student learning that provide the framework for guiding students to become lifelong seekers and responsible users of information, as defined in *Information Power: Building Partnerships for Learning* (American Library Association, 1998). The nine standards are divided into three categories: **Information Literacy, Independent Learning**, and Social Responsibility. They can be located **online** at the **AASL** Website: <http://www.ala.org/aasl>.

## Information Process Models

A series of steps used to develop students' information-seeking skills by teaching them how to define information needs, answer questions, and solve problems. There are several **information process models** from which to choose, including, the **Big6**™ Process Model, developed by Michael Eisenberg and Bob Berkowitz; Carol Kahthau's Information Problem-Solving; Barbara Stripling and Judy Pitt's Research Process; Pathways to Knowledge, and Inquiry Learning by Marjorie Pappas and Ann Tepe; and FLIP-IT by Alice Yucht.

# I

### Information Services Director

The person assigned to operate and maintain a host of computers within the school district or business. Sometimes referred to as a systems operator, **network** manager, or information technology director.

### Ink-Jet Printer

A nonimpact printer that applies ink dots through jets onto the paper.

### Integrated Software

Computer program that contains several different complete applications within one package. Word processing, **database**, and **spreadsheet** programs are examples.

### Intellectual Freedom

The right to read, view, and listen to whatever an individual chooses. The Intellectual Freedom policy statement can be accessed **online** from the **American Library Association**: <http://www.ala.org/> and the **AASL** Website: <http://www.ala.org/aasl/>.

### Interactive

A computer application or system in which the user can enter a command or question and expect a reply or answer.

### Interlibrary Loan (ILL)

A systematic method of sharing **resources** between different libraries. See also: *Document Delivery*.

### International Society for Technology in Education (ISTE)

A nonprofit organization composed of members who are leaders in educational **technology**. Provides services and leadership dedicated to improving teaching and learning by promoting the effective use of **technology** in K-12 education and teacher education programs. Information is available at <http://www.iste.org>.

## International Standard Bibliographic Description (ISBD)

A standard format for inserting specific punctuation marks in the bibliographic description of an item that tells the computer exactly where to place particular pieces of information within that **bibliographic record**. Punctuation standardization allows the information to transcend language barriers. If a person does not understand a language, but recognizes the meaning of the punctuation marks, he or she will know what type of information is contained within those symbols, such as if it is the **title**, **author**, or another piece of information about that item.

## International Standard Book Number (ISBN)

The unique ten-digit number assigned to every printed book prior to publication. Using the ISBN when searching for an item in the **online catalog** retrieves only that particular item. It permits more efficient ordering, **inventory** control, and accounting. Numbers are assigned in the following order to identify:

>The national, geographic, language, or other group.
>The **publisher** or producer.
>The **title**.
>The check digit (used to detect transcription errors).

## International Standard Serial Number (ISSN)

The unique eight-digit number assigned to each published **serial**.

## International Standards Organization (ISO)

Founded in 1946, it promotes and defines standardization of the computer, communication **protocols**, and related **fields**. The most significant contribution of this organization may be the Open Systems Interconnection (OSI), which is a standardized architecture for designing **networks**. Members include national standards organizations from over 75 countries. American National Standards Institute (ANSI) is the United States section of the organization.

## Internet

An international **network** of linked computers using **TCP/IP protocol** that makes the sharing of information possible over the **World Wide Web** and through **email** and newsgroups.

## Internet Service Provider (ISP)

A fee-based service that offers a portal through which one can connect to the **Internet** via computer and telecommunication devices.

# I

### Intranet

The **network** of computers connected within a limited area, such as a business, organization, or school district.

### Inventory

A check of the library media center's **holdings** against a **shelflist** or electronic **catalog record** to determine what items are missing from the collection. Automated circulation systems have a component that performs this task. A **personal digital assistant (PDA)** can further streamline this process. The PDA can be taken directly to the shelf to scan **barcodes** on items and automatically input the information into the **circulation software system**.

### JPEG
See *Joint Photographic Expert Group.*

### Java
Developed by Sun Microsystems, this programming language allows **multimedia** to be incorporated into **Web** pages.

### Jobber
A business that purchases materials from the **publisher** or producer and in turn sells the products to the customer. The jobber may do some second-level work with the material before submitting it to the customer for purchase, such as reinforcing the binding. It affords a customer the opportunity to purchase a variety of materials from several producers and **publishers** at possibly discounted prices.

### Joint Author
One who has worked with another person(s) to create a specific work.

### Joint Photographic Expert Group (JPEG)
An algorithm used to compress images, allowing faster transmission over telecommunication lines.

# J

## Journal

A **periodical** issued on a regular basis, for example, weekly, monthly or annually. It is usually intended for readers interested in a particular discipline. Considered to be more scholarly than a general/popular **magazine**, articles often contain footnotes and/or bibliographic **references** and are often subject to peer or editorial committee review.

# K

In computer terminology, K=1024 **bytes** of memory.

## Key Heading

A set of subdivisions in *Sears* that provides an example of terms used to construct similar **headings**. For example, instead of including the sub-headings to be used with each of the 50 states, the **heading** for California is used as the key heading.

## Keyword Searching

Directs the computer to locate a word or phrase in a **cataloging record** or **database**. Expands searches by picking up words from several areas of a **bibliographic record**, such as the **annotation**, notes, etc. **Search engines** on the **Internet** allow the user to use **natural language** when searching. **Boolean** logic can be used to limit the number of hits and improve the relevancy of the returns. See also: *Booleen Searching*.

## Knowledge Quest

A **periodical** of American Association of School Libraries **AASL**. Published bimonthly, September through June, and distributed to members. It covers topics and issues of interest to the school library media community. The **online** version is available to members and subscribers.

## LAN
See *Local Area Network*.

## LC
See *Library of Congress*.

## LCC
See *Library of Congress Classification*.

## LCCN
See *Library of Congress Control Number*.

## LCSH
See *Library of Congress Subject Headings*.

## LM_NET
A national **Listserv** for school library media personnel. Visit <http://www.eduref.org/lm_net/> to subscribe to the **Listserv**.

## Laser Disc
An optical, **digital** storage medium read by a compatible player that is rapidly being replaced by the smaller, more efficient **DVD** format.

# L

### Laser Printer
A nonimpact device that places images and text on a rotating drum using a ruby laser beam that charges the surface of the paper for the formation of print. Dry toner adheres to the paper and is heat-fused, producing a better quality of print than a **dot matrix** or **ink jet printer**.

### Lesson Plan
A carefully designed sequence of educational instruction, containing objectives, **resources** required, presentational/instructional strategies, an **assessment** plan, and an **evaluation**. Classroom teachers are required to develop lesson plans as part of their teaching responsibilities. **Library media specialists** must plan their own instructional strategies, including clearly defined objectives and an **evaluation** of their plan.

### Letter-by-Letter Alphabetization
Alphabetizing system that ignores the spaces between words, used primarily by dictionary-type publications to keep compound words together. See also: *Word-by-Word Alphabetization*.

### Librarian
A person holding a master's degree or credential from an accredited university offering an MLS, MLIS, and/or a school library media credential. Those employed to work in a school library frequently hold a teaching credential as well as a library media services credential. Persons seeking employment as public school **library media specialists** should check with the department of education in their state for specific credential requirements.

### Library Bill of Rights
A statement regarding **intellectual freedom** from the **American Library Association**. It states that, " …all libraries are forums for information and ideas…" and offers six basic guidelines to implement the policies. For the full version of the statement, go to <http://ala.org>.

### Library Binding
Reinforcing a book; making it strong enough to withstand heavy use. Though some **publishers** offer this type of binding on their books, the term often indicates a **jobber** or **vendor** has rebound the book.

## Library Clerk
A paraprofessional who performs the clerical tasks involved in the library program. See also: *Library Technician*.

## Library Media Plan
A three or five-year design for the library media program. Should be a collaborative effort between library media personnel and members of the school community, such as teachers, administrators, parents, and students. When completed, it is presented to the district's governing body for adoption, which provides an ideal opportunity for spotlighting the library program.

## Library Media Specialist (LMS)
A person holding a specific credential from an accredited university. Also called Library Media Teacher (LMT) or Teacher Librarian (TL), depending on the geographic area. See also: *Librarian*.

## Library of Congress (LC)
The United States national library. It began with the acquisition of Thomas Jefferson's collection of books and is now the largest library in the world, containing more than 120 million items. The library exists to serve the Congress and the American people. Besides the myriad **resources** available, it offers a vast array of services and support for citizens of all ages. Explore this "mother of all libraries" at <http://www.loc.gov/>.

## Library of Congress Classification System (LCC)
Designed by the **LC** and used by most academic, research, and other large libraries, the system divides materials into subject areas. Call numbers begin with one to three letters, followed by various combinations of whole numbers, decimal numbers, and/or more letters. These are then followed by the year of publication.

## Library of Congress Subject Headings (LCSH)
A system of **controlled vocabulary** specifying what term(s) to use to describe the contents of a work. Large academic libraries use LCSH. Schools and other small libraries may prefer to use **Sears Subject Heading**, which holds more relevance for students and the general public.

# L

### Library Technician
A paraprofessional in the library who deals with the **technical services** of operating a library center. The library technician often has earned a certificate or associate degree from an accredited community college program. See also: *Library Clerk*.

### Listserv
An **email**-based message system to which users may subscribe, allowing them to receive and post messages to each other. A single message can be simultaneously delivered to a large number of **email** addresses.

### Local Area Network (LAN)
A **network** contained within a particular physical site. A school, business, or home can share information and resources such as printers and CD towers over a LAN.

### Location
The area in the library where a physical item can be found. The call or **classification number** points the **patron** to where the item(s) is located, in much the same way as an address points to a business or home.

### Log In/Log Out
Initiating and terminating a session on a networked **server**.

### Lossy Compression
Data **compression** technique for converting large files and graphics into smaller formats for more efficient storage and to facilitate faster transmission.

### Lurker
Someone who subscribes to a discussion group, such as a **Listserv**, reads the messages posted, but does not participate in the discussion.

### MARC
See *Machine Readable Cataloging*.

### Machine Readable Cataloging (MARC)
A uniform system of codes established by the **LC** that allows **bibliographic records** to be created in an electronic format that can then be read by a computer **software** program. Use of the standardized MARC format promotes the electronic sharing of **resources** and information and makes the library **catalog** available to users via the **OPAC**.

### Magazine
A **periodical** written more for the general public than for those interested in scholarly pursuits. It is published on a regular basis (weekly, monthly, or annually).

### Main Entry Card
The basic, or unit, **record** from which other **catalog cards** are made. Typically, the **author card** is designated as the main entry card. In an **OPAC** system, the concept of main entry is irrelevant.

### Manuscript
An **author's** work before it is published.

# M

### Marketing
Promoting the services and **resources** of the library media center to students, faculty, administrators, and the community.

### Media
The physical material that stores data. **Floppy disks**, hard disks, and **Zip disks** are magnetic **media**, similar to audio and videotape, while **CD-ROMs, DVDs,** and old **Laser Discs** are optical **media** written upon and read by laser light.

### Megabyte
Approximately one million **bytes** or 1024 x 1024 **bytes**.

### Menu
The display screen on a computer that offers the user a number of choices to **access** additional information. A mouse or keyboard may be used to activate the menu options.

### Microfiche
A **microfilm,** in sheet form, on which greatly reduced images of many pages are reproduced. Special readers are required to view and print the information.

### Microfilm
Magnetic **media** on which **periodicals** and other documents are reproduced for long-term storage.

### Microform
A term used to describe a method of preservation of materials in a reduced format. It can refer to **microfiche** or **microfilm**. Special machines are required to **access** the information. **Digitization** of materials is gradually taking the place of this method of preservation.

### *Middle and Junior High School Library Catalog*
An H.W. Wilson publication that includes an extensive list of good quality materials for children. This resource is widely used as a general selection tool. Others in the **series** are: *Children's Catalog* and *Senior High School Library Catalog*. All are now available in electronic format and **online**.

# M

## Modem
Acronym for MOdulator-DEModulator, an external or internal computer device that interprets and translates incoming and outgoing signals into appropriate format, transmitted via **telecommunication** facilities.

## Monograph
A complete one-**volume** book. Can be used synonymously for book.

## Monographic Series
A set of **monographs** published under a collective **title**.

## Moving Picture Expert Group (MPEG)
A group of **ISO** who developed **compression** standards and formats for converting video to **digital** images for manipulation and transmission that can be decoded by **software** and special **hardware**.

## Multimedia
A presentation, transmission, or program that incorporates several **media**: text, graphics, sound, etc.

### National Board for Professional Teaching Standards (NBPTS)
An organization that awards national certification for teachers who successfully pass several subject matter tests and complete an extensive portfolio, which includes documentation of community involvement and outreach, a written analysis of student work, and a classroom video demonstrating exceptional teaching practices. States and districts often offer financial incentives for teachers seeking and achieving the certification. In 2002, **library media specialists** were invited to apply for national board certification.

### National Council for the Accreditation of Teacher Education (NCATE)
A national consortium that provides **accreditation** to colleges of education offering a school **library media specialist** degree. Schools are judged against a rigorous set of standards designed to assure that candidates are fully prepared to meet the challenges of actively engaging students in learning.

### National Information Standards Organization (NISO)
An organization devoted to the development and use of standards in information services, libraries, and the publishing world.

### Natural Language
The ability to use phrases and sentences (not **keywords**) to conduct searches in an **OPAC** or with **Internet search engines**.

# N

### Netiquette
An unwritten code of manners and behaviors covering conduct over the **Internet**. For instance, one should not forward an individual's email message without first asking permission.

### Network
A group of computers set up to communicate with one another. A **LAN** or a **wide area network (WAN)** are examples. The **Internet** is made up of thousands of individual **networks**.

### Network Printer
A printer capable of accepting and printing data from several computers on a **work station** or through an **Intranet**.

### No Child Left Behind Act of 2001 (NCLB)
A national initiative embraced by President George W. Bush to promote excellence in our schools. Enacted in 2001, it reauthorized **ESEA**. It promotes increased **accountability**, particularly for low-performing schools, and grants greater flexibility to local educational agencies. Early reading literacy is a major focus. Improving Literacy Through School Libraries is an extension of the Act. Districts and schools may apply for a grant for funding under this option. Information on NCLB can be found at< http://www.ed.gov/nclb/landing/jhtml>.

### Nonbook Materials
Library materials not in print format, such as globes, videotapes, **CD-ROMs**, and **realia**.

### Non-Circulating Items
A library item that is not checked out, but is instead kept in the library. There are several types of non-circulating items, such as books for **reference** use, some popular high-use periodicals and **journals**, and one-of-a-kind and/or irreplaceable materials.

## OCLC
See *Online Computer Library Center*.

## OPAC
See *Online Public Access Catalog*.

## OCLC WorldCat
An **online union catalog** holding **bibliographic records** for books, **journals**, and other materials of member libraries. Members may use this bibliographic **database** for **copy cataloging** or **interlibrary loan**.

## Online
The **synchronous** or real-time communication link between the user and a computer **network**.

## Online Catalog
Also called the **online public access catalog** (**OPAC**). A computerized **software** system that replaces the **card catalog** for accessing materials in a particular library or group of libraries. The computer is programmed to display enough information on **resources** for **patrons** to determine the subject, where it is located on the shelf, and if it is available for checkout.

# O

### Online Computer Library Center (OCLC)
An international, cooperative, **online** bibliographic **network** containing the **union catalog holdings** of a number of libraries. Offers a variety of fee-based services including a subscription service to *FirstSearch*, an amalgamation of scholarly **electronic databases**.

### Online Learning
Using the **Internet** to provide **interactive** educational opportunities. Several commercial services offer structures for **online** learning modules, such as Blackboard and eCollege. **Online** learning may involve both **asynchronous** and **synchronous** interaction among classmates, instructors, and **curriculum**.

### Online Public Access Catalog (OPAC)
Electronic **records** of library **holdings**, replacing the print or card file. **Resources** can be viewed via a computer **terminal**, permitting users to search by subject, **title**, **author**, and **keyword**. **Patrons** can determine if an item is in the library or checked out, where it can be found on the shelves, and information on the contents.

### Online Reference
Materials accessed by electronic means, such as the **Internet** or on **CD-ROM** discs. It may also refer to **synchronous** or **asynchronous access** to a reference **librarian** service via the **Internet**.

### Operating System
Compute**r software** that controls the functions of other programs and the **CPU**.

### Original Cataloging
The process of creating a new **bibliographic record** for a library item. See also: *Copy Cataloging*.

### Out of Print (OP)
A book no longer **in print** and not available for purchase from the **publisher**. **Titles** may possibly still be obtained using the services of book dealers specializing in locating these books.

### PDF
See *Portable Document Format.*

### POP
See *Post Office Protocol.*

### PPP
See *Point to Point Protocol.*

### Pagination
Numbers or letters used to designate the order and number of pages. In the **physical description area** of the **cataloging record**, it indicates the number of pages in that particular book.

### Parallel Port
The interface is found on the back of a computer used for connecting external devices, such as printers or scanners. It uses a 25-pin connector (DB-25) and is rather large compared to most new interfaces. The USB and Firewire interfaces are replacing the parallel port.

### Patron
Library user/borrower.

# P

## Patron Record
Pertinent information about a person borrowing materials from the library.

## Periodical
A publication appearing at regular intervals and numbered in successive issues or parts.

## Periodical Index
The guide to the contents of a large number of **periodicals**. Can be arranged in a variety of ways, such as by **author, title**, or subject. May focus on a particular subject or cover a variety of topics. Today periodical indices are best described as **databases**, and most are accessed electronically. **Online databases** may provide **access** to **citations, citations** with **abstracts**, or **full text** of items included in the **database**.

## Peripheral Equipment
Internal or external devices that communicate directly with the **CPU**. For example, printers, **DVDs**, and projection devices.

## Personal Author
The person responsible for the creation of a work.

## Personal Digital Assistant (PDA)
A hand-held organizer, which contains a datebook, address files, and other services. For libraries, an enhanced PDA can be used to scan the shelves and import the data into a computer to conduct an **inventory** of the library's **resources**.

## Physical Description Area
The fifth area of the bibliographic description in a **bibliographic record**. It describes the physical parts of a work. In the **record** for a book, it should provide information on the number of pages, dimensions and illustrations.

## Plagiarism
Using materials created by others without giving credit to the creator. The **Internet** makes this easier as students can simply copy and paste the information into their document. **Information literate** students possess the skills for conducting original **research** and understand the importance of properly citing their sources.

# P

### Platform
A computer's **operating system**, such as, Windows, Mac, UNIX, Linux, or DOS.

### Point to Point Protocol (PPP)
A **protocol** allowing computers to access and transmit over the **Internet** via a telephone line and a **modem**.

### Portable Document Format (PDF)
Developed by Adobe, it allows documents containing graphics and fonts to be converted and displayed in their original layout when transmitted over the **Internet**. Documents in PDF format require **Adobe Acrobat Reader** to display the documents.

### Post Office Protocol (POP)
A program allowing incoming **email** to be retrieved from a remote computer.

### Prebound
Books reinforced with a special heavy-duty binding at the time of publication.

### Preface
The beginning part of a book that states the **author's** purpose and vision for creating the work.

### Preprocessing
Preparing items to reach the library ready to be shelved and circulated. This may be a service supplied by a **publisher**, **jobber**, or producer. Items should arrive processed according to predetermined specifications. For example, they may be cataloged and covered with a plastic jacket, with spine and **barcode** labels attached in the proper places. Definitive specification indigenous to a particular library must be clearly conveyed to the processor to ensure that the items arrive correctly prepared and ready to be used.

### Primary Source
Original **manuscripts**, documents, speeches, letters, diaries, or other items created at the time an event(s) occurred. The **American Memory Project** of the **LC** provides an excellent array of primary sources. It can be accessed at <http://memory.loc.gov/>.

# P

### Processing Center
The area at a school or district where incoming materials are processed for a group of libraries. In schools, this could be handled at the district office level and may include the ordering of materials.

### Prompt
A message or symbol appearing on the computer screen, which asks for input from the user.

### Protocol
A formal set of rules governing the format and timing of electronic messages, permitting different types of computers to communicate with each other.

### Public Domain Software
A free computer **application** frequently downloaded from the **Internet** that is not **copyrighted**.

### Public Relations
Projecting a positive image of the library to the school and community through activities and programs designed to enhance, and perhaps change, the perception of the school library program. See also: *Marketing* and *Advocacy*.

### Publication and Distribution Area
The fourth area of the bibliographic description that tells who, when, and where the item was published or produced.

### Publisher
The person, company, or corporation responsible for printing and issuing material.

### Pupil-Teacher Ratio
The total student enrollment divided by the number of full-time equivalent teachers. The pupil-teacher ratio is a common statistic for comparing schools.

### Push Technology
The delivery of information over the **Internet** supplied by a **client** program from information previously gathered by that **server**. It allows companies to provide information—via the computer screen—not requested by the user.

## Qualifier
A word or phase, usually in parentheses, that clarifies the **access point**.

## Qualitative Measures
Methods used in the **evaluation** and **assessment** of the school library program. Observation and interviews yield qualitative data that is then analyzed to identify trends or patterns. Qualitative measures provide insight into the substance or quality of a program or its **resources**. See also: *Quantitative Measures*.

## Quantitative Measures
Methods used in the **evaluation** and **assessment** of the school library program. Circulation statistics, counts of the number of class visits to the media center, and frequency of use of the **OPAC** are examples of quantitative measures. Quantitative measures can be used to generate a statistical picture of use. See also: *Qualitative Measures*.

## Quarterly
A **periodical** published four times a year.

### Random Access Memory (RAM)
The temporary computer memory available. Information held in RAM is lost when the computer is turned off.

### Read-Only Memory (ROM)
Storage device built into computer **hardware** that cannot be altered by the user. It is used to operate **software** and resides as permanent memory on the computer's hard drive.

### Readers Advisory
The art of assisting **patrons** in their quest to locate library materials, usually for pleasure reading. Library personnel depend on knowledge of their **patron's** interests and ability level to effectively assist them in locating materials.

### Reading Shelves
Verifying proper arrangement of materials on the bookshelf according to their **classification** or **call number.** Can be done by trained, responsible students or parent volunteers.

### Ready Reference
Materials used to quickly provide an answer to a simple information need or question. It also refers to the type of question that can be answered quickly by consulting a single source.

# R

### Realia
Real objects, **artifacts**, or specimens, such as a bird's nest.

### Rebinding
The process of reconditioning worn books by trimming, resewing, and adding new covers.

### Record
A single **entry** in a **database**. A complete **catalog** record would consist of the **author, title**, date, **publisher, subject headings**, and **annotation**. See also: *Bibliographic Record*.

### Recreational Reading
Reading materials simply for the pleasure derived from the activity.

### Recto
The right hand page of a book or the front of a single sheet. The **title page** is usually on the recto. It is opposite the **verso** page.

### Refereed Journal
A scholarly **journal** containing articles that have been accepted for publication following a review by a panel of peers knowledgeable about the subject or topic.

### Reference
A service provided by library personnel to assist the **patron** in the retrieval and use of information **resources**. Also refers to the area in the library where **reference materials** are located, to the instruction in a **catalog** that directs users to another **catalog entry**, and to the listing of sources in an article or book.

### Reference Desk
The service area of the library where **patrons** can request help with using the library and assistance with information needs. In most school libraries this also doubles as a **circulation desk**. The reference area should encourage **patrons** to seek assistance by being prominently located and maintaining a welcoming atmosphere.

# R

### Reference Interview
The questioning conducted by a **librarian** to determine a **patron's** informational needs. A skilled **librarian** can guide the **patron** toward asking the right questions in order to **access** relevant information.

### Reference Materials
**Resources** available on a variety of topics and in the proper format with the potential of fulfilling informational needs. These **resources** are typically not circulated, but are kept in the library for **access** by those doing **research** in the library. Could include dictionaries, **encyclopedias**, indices, and other factual types of materials, including **online** and **electronic resources**.

### Reinforced Editions
Trade **editions** of books that have been more securely sewn and bound into stronger covers.

### Remote Access
Accessing information through an off-site computer from a place other than the school library. The library Web page can be a portal through which students can log on from home to **access** the **OPAC** or other **online databases**.

### Reprint
Reissuing of a book that may have gone **out of print**.

### Request for Proposal (RFP)
To invite companies to submit a bid for outside services, major materials, and/or equipment. Most school districts state that items and services over a certain amount of money require schools to initiate this process. For instance, items over $15,000 may require soliciting bids from several companies. This amount varies from district to district. RFP also refers to the requirements specified when a grant proposal is prepared. For example, many state departments of education regularly publish RFPs to determine how technological funds will be distributed and spent. Local schools and/or districts then compete for the funds available by preparing proposals following guidelines in the RFP.

### Research
The process of seeking information to solve problems.

# R

### The Research Libraries Information Network (RLIN)
An information management and retrieval system. Hundreds of research libraries, repositories, and museums contributed to building this international **database** of bibliographic information for scholarly **research**.

### Reserve Collection
Books or articles being held in the library to use for a pending classroom assignment.

### Resource-Based Learning
A student-centered method of inquiry. Students use a wide range of appropriate **resources** to facilitate their own learning, guided by a **library media specialist**. Through proper instruction, they become creative problem-solvers, independent learners, and active seekers of knowledge and understanding.

### Resources
Materials in print, **electronic**, **multimedia**, and **online** formats, within and without the library collection. They are selected to provide factual, interesting, pertinent, and enjoyable information to the user.

### Retrospective Conversion
Transferring library **records** from print to electronic—**MARC**—format. **Records** are standardized using the **MARC** format to enable **access** through a computerized **automation system**. See also: *Machine Readable Cataloging*.

### Router
A **hardware** device that selects the most effective path in a **network** and transmits the information accordingly.

### Rule of Three
A library term used to instruct the cataloger on how to **catalog** an item that has multiple creators or subjects. It states that if three or more people are equally responsible for the creation of a work, catalogers would then use the **title** of the work as the **main entry**. The same rule applies to **cataloging** and classifying subjects.

### SMTP
See *Simple Mail Transfer Protocol*.

### Scanner
A device used to reproduce a text or graphic into computer language that then can be manipulated and edited by a computer **software** program.

### School Interoperability Framework
A set of common definitions and rules for sharing school data developed by a non-profit organization consisting of vendors, governmental agencies, state departments of education, and other industry leaders. The specifications allow software applications from different vendors to seamlessly interact and share data regardless of the kind of computer or networks being used.

### Scope
The depth and breadth of a particular resource used in assessing the intrinsic value of the work.

### Search Engine
**Software** that allows users to search **databases** of Web **resources** to retrieve information. Some search engines permit **Boolean searching**, which can be used to limit the number of hits, allowing for more relevant results.

# S

### Search Strategy
The process of knowing, using, and/or developing the most expedient method for locating the most pertinent information.

### Sears List of Subject Headings (Sears)
A **controlled vocabulary** of terms and phrases used to assign **access points** to library materials. This **thesaurus** is the one most commonly used by school and small public libraries because the language is more appropriate for the general public and students.

### Secondary Source
This type of resource builds upon the original or **primary source**. It is not in the original form, but has been interpreted, adapted, commented on, or critiqued by another.

### "See" or "See also" Reference
A guide to another or related term that extends a search. See also: *Cross-Reference*.

### Selection Policy
Establishes the procedures for selecting library **resources**. In addition to offering detailed methods for the selection of **resources**, it also should contain instructions on dealing with material challenges and the **weeding** and discarding of library materials. The policy should be districtwide and approved by the district's governing body.

### Selection Tools
**Resources** from which to select appropriate materials for the library media center. The best selection tools provide an evaluative review and a synopsis of the content to assist in the selection of appropriate materials. There are multiple types of **journals**, books, and electronic sources used for this purpose. Some of the more common **journals** for selecting library **resources** are *Library Media Connection, School Library Journal, Horn Book,* and *Booklist*.

### *Senior High School Library Catalog*
An H.W. Wilson publication that includes an extensive list of good quality materials for young adults. This resource is widely used as a general **selection tool**. Others in the **series** are: *Children's Catalog* and *Middle and Junior High School Library Catalog*. All are now available in electronic format and **online**.

## Serial

A publication issued successively in parts, regularly or irregularly, and intended to continue indefinitely. Examples include **periodicals**, newspapers, **almanacs**, or reports.

## Serial Port

A connector on a computer for attaching **peripheral equipment**, such as external **modems**, printers, and **scanners**.

## Series

A group of **monographs** on the same subject or theme, published under a common subject and **title**, but with different **subtitles**. Also, the sixth area of the **bibliographic record** dealing with series information. In **MARC records,** it is recorded in MARC **tags** 4XX and 830. For example, *America the Beautiful* is a series on the individual states and *Nancy Drew* is a series of fictional works.

## Server

A computer, usually more powerful than a standard personal computer, that sends data or services to **clients**.

## Shared Responsibility

The part of the **bibliographic record** that recognizes the joint efforts of creating a work when both parties contribute equally to its creation. An example of this would be recognizing the work of both the **author** and illustrator in the creation of a picture book.

## Shareware

**Software** offered for a free trial from sources such as the **Internet**. After a trial period, the user is asked to send a fee to the developer to continue to use it or to unlock additional features.

## Shelflist

A **record** on 3"x5" cards of all materials in the collection filed by **classification number** as they appear on the shelf, with each card representing a single **title**. The shelflist file is used by the library staff and represents the **inventory** of that library. The **online catalog** has largely replaced the need for these cards.

# S

### Shelving
The place on which library materials are stored. Also refers to putting materials back on the shelves when they are returned to the library.

### Simple Mail Transfer Protocol (SMTP)
The **Internet** standard **protocol** for transferring **email** messages between computers; used for outgoing **email** messages.

### Site-Based Management
Also called School-Based Management, it is part of a movement to empower teachers and other instructional staff in the decision-making at the school site. Decisions dealing with **curriculum**, budget, staff development, and other school issues are made at the site instead of being made by the superintendent or the governing board.

### Software
The set of instructions that tell the computer what tasks to perform. Can be found on many **media**, such as **floppy disks**, **CD-ROMs**, or on **ROM** chips.

### Software Licensing
A permit purchased from a **software** company granting use of their **application program** on a specified number of individual computers at the school site or districtwide.

### Spam
Annoying and unsolicited **email** messages.

### Special Collection
A group of **resources** stored together and built around a certain subject or theme.

### Special Education
Programs that identify and attempt to meet the educational needs of children with emotional, learning, or physical disabilities. Federal law requires that all children with exceptionalities—from infancy to age 21—be provided a free and appropriate education according to an Individual Education Plan (IEP). Library media personnel develop programs and **resources** to assure equal **access** for all.

## Spreadsheet
A computer application that allows for the creation and use of accounting type documents, with columns and rows of figures and text that can be manipulated by the user.

## Stacks
The area in the library where materials are shelved. Appropriate signage facilitates use of this the library.

## Standard Number and Terms of Availability Area
The eighth area of the **bibliographic record**, which includes the **ISBN** or **ISSN** numbers and when appropriate, the price of the item; can be found in **MARC tags** 01X—09X.

## Statement of Responsibility
The first area of the **bibliographic record** that names those responsible for the creation of the item. It correlates to **MARC tags** 1XX, 245, 246, and 7XX. See also: *Title and Statement of Responsibility Area*.

## Statistical Abstracts
The geographic or political statistics of an area.

## Streaming Video
Video file transmitted via the **Internet** and viewed as it is received.

## Study Print
A picture, dealing with a specific subject or theme, used for instructional purposes.

## Style Guide
Publication(s) that provide rules and guidance for citing and referencing materials in a document, for example, *Modern Language Association* (MLA) and *American Psychological Association* (APA).

## Subfield Codes
A content-designated segment of a **field** in a **MARC record**; usually a lower case letter, preceded by a **delimiter** that separates the subfields.

# S

### Subject Card
A rectangular piece of stiff paper in the **catalog** drawer with the subject on the top line. This is always typed in capital letters.

### Subject Cataloging
Assigning the proper **subject heading(s)** and **classification number** to an item. It requires the cataloger to peruse enough of a work to accurately determine the subject matter and use **authority control files** to correctly complete the process.

### Subject Heading
**Controlled vocabulary** used to indicate the topic of the material. Using **authority control** lists assures that materials are readily accessible to the user. Most libraries use the **LCSH**, *Sears*, or the **AC** subject headings.

### Subtitle
A secondary word or phrase, following the main **title**, which is sometimes used to explain, limit, or expand the **title** proper.

### Sustained Silent Reading
A specific time set aside for the school—students, staff, and faculty—to stop all other activities and read.

### Synchronous
Occurring at the same time. In the **online** world, users would be communicating in real-time. This would most likely be in an **online** chat room or using instant messaging.

### Syndetic Structure
This refers to the "**see**" and "**see also**" **cross reference** system used to point **patrons** to other or additional **resources**.

### System Upgrade
Purchasing a new version of a particular piece of **software** or **hardware**.

## TCP/IP
See *Transmission Control Protocol/Internet Protocol*.

## Tag
A three-character numeric code that identifies a **field** in a **MARC record**. Each **field** in a **MARC record** is identified by this code. For example, the 100 tag usually contains a personal name or group responsible for the intellectual content, but a **uniform title** may also be found in this area if it is a **main entry**.

## Technical Services
The part of the library program that deals with the **acquisition**, **cataloging**, record-keeping, and physical preparation of materials.

## Technology
The practical application of science, referred to here as the vast array of machines, tools, and applications that allow schools, governments, associations, and businesses to operate more quickly and efficiently.

## Technology Coordinator
The person who oversees the selection, purchase, operation, maintenance, and disposal of a school or district's **hardware**, **software**, and **network** and is responsible for their proper functioning.

# T

### Technology Literacy
Understanding and using the complex **software** and **hardware** associated with computers and **multimedia** and integrating it into other **resources** associated with teaching and learning.

### Telecommunications
Electronic systems used to communicate information from one point to another either by microwave, telephone, or radio.

### Teleconferencing
Using video and audio devices to communicate and teach in real-time from a distance.

### Terminal
A monitor and keyboard lacking a **CPU**; used for data entry and to display information from a mainframe computer. An **OPAC** is often accessed through a computer terminal.

### Thesaurus
A dictionary that provides lists of synonyms and antonyms. Also, a specialized **authority file** of terms, such as **subject headings** or descriptors used in an automated retrieval system for a particular **database**, **catalog**, or **index**. The **LCSH** and *Sears* are considered thesauruses.

### Thesis
An original **research** paper written by a candidate for an academic degree.

### Title
The name assigned to a work, usually identified from the **chief source of information** of an item.

### Title I, Migrant Education
Federal funds allocated specifically to help districts/schools meet the special needs of students whose parents are migrant workers. Library media personnel should support this program by providing materials in the library to enhance these efforts. Information on this and other federal education programs can be found at <http://www.ed.gov/>.

## Title I, Title VI

Funds from the Federal Educational Consolidation and Improvement Act. Title I is designated for educationally disadvantaged children; Title VI is for innovative education program strategies (the names of these types of programs frequently change under new leadership). Information on these and other federal education programs can be found at the Department of Education **Web site** <http://www.ed.gov/>.

## Title and Statement of Responsibility Area

The first area of a bibliographic description. It includes the **title** and information on the creator(s) of the work. Corresponds to the **MARC tags** 1XX, 245, 246, and 7XX. See also: *Statement of Responsibility*.

## Title Card

A rectangular piece of stiff paper in the **catalog** drawer with the **title** on the top line.

## Title Page

The first part of a book where the **title, author** and publication information is provided.

## Title Proper

The descriptive name of an item.

## Tome

A **volume** that is part of several in a work, especially a lengthy or scholarly one.

## Tracing

A notation on a **card catalog record** identifying additional **subject heading, joint authors**, illustrators, and other terms under which the item is listed.

## Trade Edition

A book typically bound for sale to the general public.

## Transformational Leadership

The ability to recognize the need for some kind of change, develop a vision to facilitate that change, then foster and model appropriate strategies to achieve a successful transformation.

# T

### Transmission Control Protocol/Internet Protocol (TCP/IP)
A set of communication **protocols** used to move information over **networks** and the **Internet**.

### Transparency
See-through material that can be used to replicate print and images for enlarged projection via an overhead projector.

### Truncation
A method of shortening a word or phrase, using a symbol (such as * or #) at the end or in the middle, to retrieve a wider variety of possibilities during a search for information on the **Internet** or in a **database**. An example would be "librar*", which would bring up library, libraries, **librarians**, or librarianship.

### Turnkey System
An automated computer system that permits flexibility in choosing its various components, resulting in a unit that meets the specific needs of a particular library.

### URL
See *Uniform Resource Locator*.

### USB
See *Universal Serial Bus*.

### Uncontrolled Vocabulary
Using any term, such as **keyword** or **natural language**, to retrieve information.

### Uniform Resource Locator (URL)
A **Web** address, the most common scheme being http. Although the term URL is better known, it has been replaced by Universal Resource Identifier (URI).

### Uniform Title
A method used to keep multiple works together, despite different **titles**, translations, and form, by using standardizing terms. For **cataloging** purposes, a specific **title** is chosen when a work appears under different **titles**. For example, all the various **editions** of Mother Goose verses would appear under the uniform title *Mother Goose*.

# U

### Uninterrupted Power Supply (UPS)
Continuous electrical currents. A battery operated device can be purchased to provide UPS in order to protect electronic information in case of a power outage. This devise assures that the computer will continue operating for a period of time, allowing for the power to be restored or for the computer to be shut down properly.

### Union Catalog
A combined listing of materials held by several libraries, which allows **patrons** to view the **holdings** in these libraries. Schools may use the union catalog to **access** other library collections within the district. It could also extend to other library **networks** outside the district. **Holdings** can also be mounted on the **Web** for **Internet** access.

### Universal Serial Bus (USB)
A standardized serial interface that allows the attachment of a number of peripherals, supports data transfer rates of 12 Mbps, and allows hot plugging (the ability to plug in a peripheral to use when the computer is running). The iMac release in 1998 caused the external bus standard to become widespread. It is expected to replace **serial** and parallel ports.

### Variable Field
An area in a **MARC record** that contains data of varying length and format.

### Vendor
A distributor who may represent a variety of **publishers** thereby facilitating the **acquisition** process. Allows libraries to consolidate orders and select from a wider variety of choices. Some may rebind books into stronger **library bindings**. See also: *Jobber*.

### Verso
The opposite of the **recto** page, it is the left-hand page of a book usually with even-numbered pages. The **copyright date** and **CIP** is most often found on this page.

### Vertical File
A collection of pamphlets, clippings, and pictures, usually housed in a filing cabinet, containing information that is transitory in nature. It often contains the most current information on a topic or locally generated material. **Technology** now allows for the possibility of creating a virtual vertical file.

# V

### Virtual Catalog
Library **resources** can be remotely accessed from a variety of points via a computer connected to the **Internet**.

### Volume
One item, unit, set, or **series**.

### WAN
See *Wide Area Network*.

### Watermark
The symbol or words faintly visible behind the words on a printed page.

### Web Browser
A graphic interface that allows connection to the **WWW** and allows the viewer to see documents as the **author** intended. Microsoft Internet Explorer and Netscape Navigator are examples of Web browsers.

### Web Site
A collection of related pages linked to a **home page** at one Web address.

### Weeding
The process of removing items from the library collection because they are no longer useful to the school community. Materials may be worn, outdated, not relevant, offensive, and/or unsuitable for student and faculty use. See also: *De-Selecting Library Materials*.

### White House Conference on School Libraries
In October 2002, First Lady Laura Bush convened this first-ever gathering of people sharing information and exploring issues pertaining to the school library community. A powerful **advocacy** program can be developed using **resources** from this conference. The tools are located at <http://www.ala.org/aasl>.

# W

### Whole Language
The theory that children learn to read, spell, and write by reading a wide variety of good literature. Subscribes to the **Constructivist Teaching** theory that learning to read is similar to learning to talk, and that children will develop literacy by reading materials in context, rather than learning words and skills in isolation. Whole language proponents promote integrating language arts into the entire **curriculum**.

### Wide Area Network (WAN)
That which links computers from two or more **local area networks (LAN)**.

### Wi-Fi
Wireless connection via high-bandwidth to networks and the Internet. Has the ability to transmit at up to 100 million bits per second, compared to a dial-up connection which communicates at 56 thousands bits per second.

### Withdrawn
An item or items removed from the collection using predetermined criteria. See also: *Weeding* and *De-Selecting Library Materials*.

### Word-by-Word Alphabetization
Alphabetizing word-by-word, not **letter-by-letter**. Spaces between words are recognized as elements. This is the method used in library **catalogs** and most **indexes**. See also: *Letter-by-Letter Alphabetization*.

### Word Processor
A computer **software** application permitting text to be keyed, spoken, or scanned into the program and then manipulated and edited with ease.

### Work Station
A computer, typically used by one person at a time, for accessing information, producing reports, or performing skill and drill exercises. Also refers to a **terminal** connected to a mainframe computer.

### World Wide Web (WWW)
A graphical **client-server** system containing millions of **hypertext** documents accessed through a computer and **telecommunications technology**. This **network** of connected **Web pages** contains text, graphics, video, and can be viewed via a **Web browser**, such as Microsoft Internet Explorer or Netscape.

### Yearbook
A publication covering information on activities and events for one particular calendar year.

### Z

### Z39.50
A standard **protocol** for designing the **software** that permits computers to communicate with each other for information retrieval and resource sharing. It allows for reciprocal **access** to other **OPACs**.

### Zip
A file **compression** format for storage and faster transmission over the **Internet**.

### Zip Disk
A storage device with the capacity to hold a large amount of data.

# Common Acronyms of Interest to Library Personnel

**AECT:** Association for Educational Communications & Technology
**AL:** *American Libraries* magazine
**ALA:** American Library Association
    **AASL:** American Association of School Librarians
        **ELMSS:** Educators of Library Media Specialists Section
        **ISS** Independent Schools Section
        **SLMR:** *School Library Media Research* (online journal)
        **SPVS:** Supervisors Section
    **ACRL:** Association of College & Research Libraries
        **RBM:** *A Journal of Rare Books, Manuscripts, and Cultural Heritage*
    **ALCTS:** Association for Library Collections & Technical Services
    **ALSC:** Association for Library Services to Children
        **JOYS:** Journal of Youth Services in Libraries
    **ALTA:** Association for Library Trustees and Advocates
    **ASCLA:** Association of Specialized and Cooperative Library Agencies
        **ICAN:** InterLibrary Cooperation Networking Section
        **ILEX:** Independent Librarian's Exchange Section
        **LSSPS:** Libraries Serving Special Populations Section
        **SLAS:** State Library Agency Section
    **LAMA:** Library Administration and Management Association
    **LITA:** Library and Information Technology Association
    **OIF:** Office of Intellectual Freedom
    **PLA:** Public Library Association
    **RBB:** *Reference Books Bulletin*
    **RUSA:** Reference and User Services Association
        **BRASS:** Business Reference and Services Section
        **CODES:** Collection Development and Evaluation Section
    **YALSA:** Young Adult Library Services Association
        **JOYS:** Journal of Youth Services in Libraries
    **WO:** Washington Office of ALA

# V

        **ALAWON:** *ALA Washington Office Electronic Newsline*
        **OGR:** Office of Government Relations
        **OITP:** Office for Information Technology Policy
**ALISE:** Association for Library and Information Science Education
**ANSI:** American National Standards Institute
**ARL:** Association of Research Libraries
**ASCD:** Association for Supervision and Curriculum Development
**ASI:** American Statistics Index
**ASIS&T:** American Society for Information Science and Technology
**CBC:** Children's Book Council
**DCMI:** Dublin Core Metadata Initiative
**DOI:** Digital Object Identifier
**ERIC:** Educational Resources Information Center
**FOLUSA:** Friends of Libraries, USA
**GEM:** Gateway to Educational Materials
**GII:** Global Information Infrastructure
**GPO:** Government Printing Office
**IFLA:** International Federation of Library Associations and Institutions
**ILS:** Integrated Library System
**IMLS:** Institute of Museum & Library Services
**IRA:** International Reading Association
**ISO:** International Organization for Standardization
**LC:** Library of Congress
      **THOMAS:** Library of Congress Federal Legislative Information Web Site
**LSTA:** Library Services and Technology Act
**NCLIS:** National Commission on Libraries & Information Science
**NCTE:** National Council of Teachers of English
      **ALAN:** Assembly on Literature for Adolescents of NCTE
**NDLF:** National Digital Library Federation
**NEH:** National Endowment for the Humanities
**NISO:** National Information Standards Organization
**NLS:** National Library Service for the Blind and Physically Handicapped
**OAI:** Open Archives Initiative
**OCLC:** Online Computer Library Center
      **PURL:** Persistent Uniform Resource Locator
      **VIAF:** Virtual International Authority File
**ONIX:** Online Information eXchange
**PADI:** Preserving Access to Digital Information

**RSS:** Really Simple Syndication
**WHCLIS:** White House Conference on Library & Information Science
**W3C:** World Wide Web Consortium

# *About the Author*

Jo Ellen Priest Misakian was awarded her Bachelor of Science degree from New York Institute of Technology and received her Library Media Teacher Services Credential and Master of Library Science degree from San Jose State University. Preferring to work part-time while raising her children, Misakian worked for many years as a library technician for Sanger Unified School District. Prior to being named director of the library media credential/master's program at Fresno Pacific University, Misakian served as library media specialist for the Fresno County Office of Education.

Misakian is past president of the California School Library Association and is currently director of Region 7 for the American Association of School Librarians. She serves on the advisory board of *Teacher Librarian*, reviews manuscripts for Linworth Publishing, and is active in several organizations in the Fresno area. She has three sons and daughters-in-law and five grandsons.

www.ingramcontent.com/pod-product-compliance
Lightning Source LLC
Chambersburg PA
CBHW051815230426
43672CB00012B/2747